Biomes

Coniferous Forests

Holly Cefrey

Rigby

Coniferous Forests
Copyright © 2002 by Rosen Book Works, Inc.

On Deck™ Reading Libraries
Published by Rigby
a division of Reed Elsevier Inc.
1000 Hart Road
Barrington, IL 60010-2627
www.rigby.com

Book Design: Mindy Liu
Text: Holly Cefrey
Photo Credits: Cover © Gunter Marx Photography/Corbis; p. 4
© MapArt, graphic by Mindy Liu; p. 5 © Michael P. Gadomski/Animals
Animals; p. 7 © Eric and David Hosking/Corbis; p. 8 © D. Robert &
Lorri Franz/Corbis; p. 9 © Tim Thompson/Corbis; pp. 10–11 © Francis
Lepine/Animals Animals; p. 12 © David Boyle/Animals Animals; p. 13
(top) © David Muench/Corbis; p. 13 (bottom) © Mike Norton/Animals
Animals; p. 15 © Tom Brakefield/Corbis; p. 16 © Charles Palek/Animals
Animals; p. 17 © Tim Zurowski/Corbis; p. 18 © Little Blue Wolf
Productions/Corbis; p. 19 © Peter Johnson/Corbis; p. 20
© Ecoscene/Corbis; p. 21 © Breck P. Kent/Animals Animals

On Deck™ is a trademark of Reed Elsevier Inc.

07 06 05
10 9 8 7 6 5 4 3

Printed in China

ISBN 0-7578-2447-1

Contents

Coniferous Forests

The coniferous forest is the largest biome on land. The coniferous forest biome is found in the northern parts of Asia, Europe, and North America.

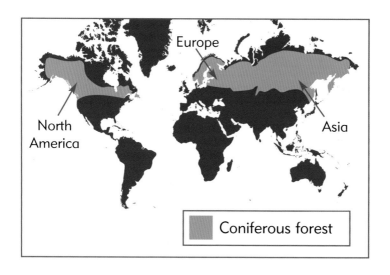

North America

Europe

Asia

Coniferous forest

Now You Know

A biome *(BY-ohm)* is a plant and animal community that covers a large part of the earth.

The coniferous forest biome makes up one-third of the world's forests.

Most of the trees in coniferous forests are conifers. Instead of growing leaves and flowers, conifers grow needles and cones. Conifers are also called evergreens. Most evergreens keep their needles or leaves all year long.

Now You Know

Conifer means "to grow cones" in the Latin language.

Most conifers grow thin needles that stay on the trees year-round.

Winters in most coniferous forests are long, cold, and snowy. Summers are usually short and warm. The temperature ranges from about −40 degrees Fahrenheit to about 68 degrees Fahrenheit (−40 degrees Celsius to 20 degrees Celsius). Most coniferous forests get about 12 to 35 inches of rain each year. Some forests get as much as 79 inches of rain a year.

The world's oldest trees are the bristlecone pines. These bristlecone pines (above) are in Colorado. One bristlecone pine in California, called Methuselah, is about 4,600 years old.

This coniferous forest is in Austria.

There are many different types of water bodies found in a coniferous forest. Some coniferous forests have bogs, shallow lakes, rivers, or wetlands. These bodies of water are important for the trees, the plants, and the animals that live there.

Bogs are wetlands that hold rainwater. Some bogs have been around for thousands of years.

10

Trees and Plants

Coniferous trees grow in shapes that help them live through cold, snowy winters. Their cone shapes do not let a lot of snow and ice stick to their branches. Snow would weigh down branches, making the branches snap off the trees. Also, the needles of conifers take in heat from the sun all year long.

Coniferous forests are also known as boreal forests. Boreal *means* "northern." They are also called taiga, *which means "marshy pine" in the Russian language.*

Many small plants grow in the coniferous forest. Some plants grow on the ground while others grow on tree trunks. Shrubs, mosses, and lichens make up much of the plant life in the coniferous forest.

The coniferous forest floor

Many coniferous trees grow thick bark that protects them during cold winters. The thick bark also protects the trees from small wildfires.

Animals in the Coniferous Forest

Many animals make their home in the coniferous forest. These animals have layers of fat, fur, or feathers to keep them warm during the winter. Some animals hibernate, or sleep, in the winter. Hibernating helps animals get through the winters when there is less food and warmth.

Siberian tigers live in the coniferous forests of northern China and Russia. They can jump 10 feet and eat up to 100 pounds of meat a day.

The coniferous forest is also home to many different birds, such as woodpeckers, ravens, owls, and hawks. Most of these birds make their homes in the branches of coniferous trees.

During the cold winter months, many animals of the forest, such as the black bear, hibernate. Other animals travel to warm places.

The grosbeak eats the seeds of conifers. When the weather gets too cold or food runs out, birds such as the grosbeak migrate, or move, to warm areas.

People and the Coniferous Forest

Small communities of people live in the coniferous forest. Many of them make their living by fishing, hunting, logging, or raising animals. People use wood from the trees to make many important things, such as paper, furniture, and houses.

Many people take vacations in the coniferous forest.

Logging companies cut down trees in the coniferous forest.

The coniferous forest can be harmed when people cut down too many trees. Many animals lose their homes when this happens. The animals often cannot find new places to live or enough food to eat.

The coniferous forest biome is important to many kinds of life.

Polluted air can cause forests all over the world to be harmed.

This tree is named General Sherman. It is a giant sequoia (sih-KWOY-uh). It is over 2,000 years old. General Sherman is 275 feet high and 103 feet around. Laws have been passed to protect trees such as this from being cut down.

Glossary

bogs (**bahgz**) lands that are wet and soggy

coniferous trees (koh-**nihf**-uhr-uhs **treez**) trees that grow cones rather than fruit or flowers; also called conifers or evergreens

hibernate (**hy**-buhr-nayt) to spend the winter in deep sleep

lichens (**ly**-kuhnz) small plants that often grow on rocks and look like moss

logging (**lawg**-ihng) cutting down trees, making them into logs, and getting them out of the forest

migrate (**my**-grayt) to move from one place to another

polluted (puh-**loot**-uhd) to have been dirtied, especially by waste material

shrubs (**shrubz**) low, bushy plants

wetlands (**weht**-landz) land that has a lot of water in the soil

Resources

Books

Taiga
by Elizabeth Kaplan
Benchmark Books (1996)

A Walk in the Boreal Forest
by Rebecca L. Johnson
Carolrhoda Books (2000)

Web Site

Enchanted Learning: Biomes and Habitats
http://www.EnchantedLearning.com/
    biomes/taiga/taiga.shtml

Index